Global Energy

By Kimmy Nelson

Nashville Flood 2010

In dedication to my wonderful parents William Perry Gerred and Martha Gerred (Marty as her friends knew her)

And in dedication to the greatest country in the world... this land that I love… America the beautiful. America means "loveable" and oh how my parents taught me to love this great nation. Only later to find that I love her for even more reasons than my parents taught me as America is a great lighthouse of the Gospel of Christ throughout all the world. America is Israel's friend and ally. My parents never taught me that.

Growing up, my parents had our big basement painted red white and blue in stars and stripes and they were also politically active in some Democratic campaigns. Mother sent me on a field trip to the State Capital of Missouri in Columbia when I was in the sixth grade.

Independent Africa

Independent Africa
By Kimmy D. Nelson

Free Africa

It should be the goal of every state and every nation to

become financially independent and free from the control of any other state or nations financial suppression. And free from any dependence to another state or nation.
By extracting the natural resources and goods from Africa and then having them manufactured for the economic global market to financially benefit Africa for their wellbeing and survival as sovereign states, region or nations will bring them financial security.

Keywords: Africa, Energy, Freedom, Colonization, Biofuel, Cassava, Sorghum. sub-Saharan Africa, South Africa, drought, starvation

Why Save Africa

It is also important to try and help Africa become financially independent as it is to try and help them end the years of hardship due to lack of irrigation and food supply. It will help restore proper health to the topography of the lands that were processed into desertification. We are only helping ourselves when we help Africa out of poverty.
This will also help end the starvation of millions of people on the continent of Africa if we can successfully turn desert lands into fields of cassava that are well irrigated and properly maintained.

And to plant new fields of sorghum in the South Africa region that will be converted into biofuel to be sold on the global economic market.
And possibly some of the cassava and some of the sorghum can be used as food and the other portions can be used for biofuel for the global economic market.

Africa Free From Poverty

We will examine how the top agriculture grown and extracted from Africa can be used in other ways besides food such as biofuel and energy for transportation. We will also look at the possibility to use the desert lands as new grounds to be irrigated and seeded for future cassava which is native to the Congo and Nigeria in the sub-Saharan Africa.

We will take the five themes of Geography and show how they can be used to help to implement these ideas into a realities. It is important to try and restore the desert waste lands of Africa to prevent future droughts, fires and floods of natural disasters that lands of desertification are prone to.

Location

The first location we will be discussing for possible biofuels and land restoration is in the sub-Saharan Africa in Nigeria is Latitude and Longitude 10.0 and 8.0 where cassava grows easily. The next location is in South Africa where sorghum can be grown and its Latitude is -27.636135500000000000 and Longitude 32.582519700000034000.

This is on the continent of Africa just below the continent of Europe. We will be looking at both of these regions; Nigeria in the sub-Saharan region and South Africa on the bottom part of the continent because Africa's best crops (cassava and sorghum) are found in those two regions. The sub-Saharan Africa is the area that is in need of land restoration to end the droughts, the fires and floods that are likely to happen in regions of high desertification as this one in Nigeria is.

Place

The continent of Africa is South of the continent of Europe. It is the world's second largest continent and the world's second largest population on a continent with over one billion people living on the continent of Africa. With over eleven and a half million square miles of land. It is home to the countries of Nigeria, Egypt, Tanzania, Morocco, Kenya, South Africa and more.

We will be exploring the sub-Saharan region on the lower part of North Eastern Africa. The region of Nigeria is in the sub-Saharan Desert of Africa where there are desert conditions, barren lands with minimal trees and shrubs and waste land areas for long stretches of miles.

The other place is in South Africa where there are shrubs and trees, other plants and vegetation that grows easily in that climate. This is a region that has been struck with the terrors of Aids, starvation and in some areas Malaria. The Congo is another area like Nigeria where cassava grows best and it is also an area of sub-Sahara Africa.

It will be important to know what type of apparel and dress is appropriate for the time of year or season that will be relevant to the traveler and to those who will be bringing in the equipment needed to implement the plans as well as those who will be working on the projects that will be addressed in this presentation. The two regions are different in climate and temperature all year round.

Movement

We will first need to utilize transportation to build roads and map out regions of the lands that are located in the desert regions in the sub-Saharan Africa regions of Nigeria, The Congo and any other regions that they would like to plant new fields of cassava to aid in the land restoration and to aid in the biofuel industry to help Africa become financially independent.

There will need to be lots road signs that are in the native tongue of the particular regions they will be working on so that the locals can easily read the maps. They will need to bring the irrigation equipment to the area lands that will be renewed with new cassava plantations.
They may not need irrigation or new wells in the other region of South Africa where they will be growing the sorghum and where they will be building the biofuel plant for the conversion of the sorghum grain into fuel for distribution into the global economic market.

And they will need transportation to bring in the water that will be used to irrigate the land. Possibly they can drill for and dig new wells that will help in the irrigation of the lands.
So they will need to bring in the drilling equipment to dig the new wells too in the sub-Saharan region of Nigeria and The Congo. And they will also need to bring in all the equipment to build the biofuel plants near by the harvest field to save time and transportation of taking the harvested cassava and sorghum to be converted into biofuel for the global economic market.

Sorghum is mainly found in South Africa. They will also need to make sure that there are roads built for bringing in all the equipment needed to plant and harvest the sorghum. They will also need roads to bring all the equipment to build the biofuel plants that will convert the sorghum and the cassava into biofuel. And they will need big fuel trucks to transport the cassava and sorghum biofuels to the global economic market too.

Though the colonizers brought great benefits to Africa and

to the rest of the world it is important for Africa to be self-sufficient with all of her own natural resources to ensure that she is not exploited by other more powerful countries in the world. It is important for all of the world's nations to be self-sufficient and free from poverty.

Region

Much of the Continent of Africa is the Sahara desert. But there are regions in the sub-Sahara desert region that can be restored into cassava plantations. Nigeria, The Congo, Cameroon, The Central African Republic, Ghana and much more of Africa are similar in the climate just South of the Sahara and that is an area that will work well to grow cassava.

And in another region where sorghum grows well is in South Africa and the regions of Botswana, and Namibia they are all in the same region in the Southern Continent of Africa where sorghum grows well.

Human Environment Interaction

We can see by the land desertification that the early colonization may have caused some of the land erosion in the areas of the sub-Sahara Africa. We also know that the nomads have adapted to the climate changes in Africa as they take their herds from place to place during the different seasons of the harsh climates there.

We see the camels in the Sahara desert regions and we know that they have adapted to the dry vast desert lands in the Sahara desert regions on the continent of Africa especially near Egypt where we have seen the camels in pictures next to the pyramids.

We also know that in the town of Gabon the Oil industry colonizers of Europe adapted to the climate there when they built the city there in Gabon into what it is today. Perhaps they have learned information that will be helpful to build up the biofuel industry with some of Africa's vegetation or by using the sorghum and the cassava.

The city of Gabon will have a lot of vital information that will help to save steps, time and money if and when Africa decides it will become energy independent and a big player in the global economic world of energy and resources as our planet turns to the wisdom of sustainability and ecofriendly environments.

References:
 http://www.biofuelsdigest.com/bdigest/tag/cassava/
                    http://businessafrica.net/africabiz/arcvol
2/is115front.php
 http://thewaterproject.org/digging-wells-in-africa-and-india-how-it-works
http://waterwellsforafrica.org/
                    http://www.africaguide.com/afmap.htm

China Clean Air, Japan & India Energy Independent

By Kimmy D. Nelson

Clean Air & Energy Independent Asia

It should be the goal of every state and every nation to become sustainable, energy independent and free from the control of any other state or nations. And it should be the goal of every nation to be free from any energy dependence to another state or nation's energy leverage. Also for every state and nation to be sustainable with clean air and clean water as a benefit of their success.

By extracting the natural gas resources from China, Japan and India for the use of natural gas operated vehicles, permanent magnetic generators and motors or electromagnetic grid operated trains for all of the major land transportation needs they will begin to have cleaner air and be more independent and sustainable at the same time. All the while the whole world will benefit because of their efforts to reduce greenhouse emissions and improve their global position as a leader in the new world of sustainability for the future survival of life on planet earth.

As they are improving their sovereign global position by becoming energy independent they will improve their financial security as well by reducing the need and cost of imported energy.

Keywords: China, Japan, India, green, greenhouse emissions, emissions, CO2, coral reef, sustainability, imported oil, air quality, ecofriendly, planet, earth

Why Clean Air For China & Why Energy Independence For Japan & India

It is important to try and help China become sustainable and ecofriendly so that they will have cleaner air and less pollution. It is also important to help India and Japan become energy independent all the while making the world a cleaner more ecofriendly environment.

India and Japan are dependent on imported crude oil. India has some natural gas resource in the Western Offshore region. Japan has very little natural gas. China is very dependent on coal and other unclean energy. We are only helping ourselves when we help others to become sustainable and ecofriendly. This will also help end the wearing of face masks or gas masks for millions of people in the nation of China and it will help India and Japan to be free from energy dependence on imported oils.

China Free From Pollution

We will expose how the thick haze over Bo Hai Bay and Yellow Sea is likely due to the industrial pollution in China. And how smog from mainland China has reached California. And how sulfur dioxide emissions have been on the decline since 2006. And how (CFC's) chlorofluorocarbons are responsible for tearing the hole in our atmosphere's protective ozone layer.

And how Anthropocene proves that mankind is responsible for saving or destroying our planet's eco system, our clean air and our clean water. And we must do our part to demand international action be taken to limit or stop all

industrial and agricultural pollutants from further
destroying our planet.

We can see how enormous quantities of industrial and
agricultural pollutants are contributing to the greenhouse
effect with their greenhouse gases, carbon dioxide (CO_2),
methane, and nitrous oxides and the environmental stresses
that they cause. And how they are also contributing to the
cause of the hole in the ozone's protective layer in earth's
atmosphere. We must now insist that complete recycling,
reusing, and reducing must be a global effort while we
reduce or completely stop any possible new industrial
pollutants from being produced.

Location

The first location is in India we will be discussing for
possible conversion all vehicles to use or convert to natural
gas, electromagnetic railroads or permanent magnetic
generators and motors for vehicles other than manual
transportation. There are already some natural gas pipe
lines next to Bombay (Mumbai) Latitude 18° 55' N, and
Longitude 72° 54' E border that ends or begins there on the
Eastern side that runs up through the North Eastern part of
India between Pakistan and Nepal that ends and begins in
Delhi.

And the location on the main island of Japan for the
beginning railroad is at Aomar Japan with a global position
of 40.8167° N, 140.7500° E Beijing China's location is
39.9139° N, 116.3917° E.

We will be looking at Beijing because it is one of the top
20 most polluted cities in China.
That natural gas pipe line in Bombay India need to be
enlarged to stretch the entire length and width of India's
borders and possibly through out several key points inside

along the railroads paths. The rail road runs all the way through every direction of India. Perhaps we can look at all the possibilities of extending the uses of the railroad system to include passenger trains and cargo trains and maybe increase the train schedules to make more runs for both passengers and for cargo. This would help reduce the nation's dependency on crude oil.

Japan's main island and her little outskirt islands as well need to start building fusion type reactors. And maybe they can focus on converting all vehicles to permanent magnetic generators and motors. This will end their need for imported crude oil for the nation of Japan and the nation of India since those two nation states are totally dependent on imported crude oil. This will also help tremendously in reducing greenhouse gases, methane, carbon dioxide (CO2) and nitrous oxides that are polluting the planet's atmosphere.

China must also changes to contribute to reversing the damages caused by their tremendous outpouring of toxins in the planet's environment. Japan and China can begin using steam engines to produce energy and heat without the toxic side effects.
They can help do this by converting some of their industrial plants to be energized by steam engines which are very efficient and a direct energy conversion. This will stop the outflow of the massive poisonous environmental hazards and still provide a way for them to continue their industrial contributions to the world.

And they can also convert some into biofuel research industries and other locations they can convert into fusion type reactor plants. If they build 30 strategically placed fusion type power plants in Tibet, Beijing, Shanghai and all across China that will be sufficient to supply energy for the entire nation of China.

One fusion power reactor could supply all the energy needs for Japan. They must also utilize all their natural gas lines and railroad stations to be the main source of transportation for their country.

Place

The place is the continent of Asia for China and Japan and the subcontinent of South Asia for India. China's natural gas is piped in through Miramar Burmese from the Bay of Bengal. Japan has some natural gas but limited. India has a supply of natural gas resource available to them through the Western Offshore regions by Mumbai high complex.

And all three countries have some railroad system already in place. India's rail system is extensive and well-connected throughout the nation. Japan's runs along the coast line in most of the country. China has an extensive railroad system too. Perhaps they can make sure they are using their railroads to do as much passenger and freight uses as
possible.

Movement

These are areas that are already supplied with railroads and with some natural gas pipe lines. However the natural gas pipe lines will need to be enlarged and increased in India. . Dr. Hans Petermann says "Fusion energy is hydrogen, nitrogen, H20 and oxygen processed at very high temperatures then maintained by stabilizing the temperature to produce a constant supply of energy 24/7 without the toxic waste that nuclear energy, coal and oil produce.

This is done in a fusion reactor that would have to be built and Dr. Hans Peterman can build it. The Germans have already got rid of most of their nuclear energy plants and they have switched to solar energy and natural gas. The fusion process has been known to scientist for many years.

A fusion reactor has to be constructed and built and Dr. Hans Petermann can build it. The fusion reactor which has been accomplished previously in Germany is great to phase out all nuclear power plants and switch over to fusion energy" Dr Hans continues by saying that this fusion reactor fusion energy supplies constant energy can be maintained by regulating the temperature. He said Japan can also do cold fusion like they've been doing by a scientist in France.

Dr. Stanley Pons in 1989-90 and Fleischmann (Fleischmann is now retired) but Pons has continued in the work in cold fusion (a chemical energy process) by using elements by low heat and changing chemicals molecular structure to get energy out.
And Dr. Hans says that Japan and India can also use permanent magnetic generators and motors can be used to run any vehicle. And Japan can use the steam engine for heat and China can use the steam engine for heat. And they can continue to use the electro magnetic train.

Region

Much of the Continent of Asia is already equipped with natural gas pipelines and railroads. And in the subcontinent of Asia in India they are well equipped with railroads and their own natural gas supply. Japan and China have had lots of interactions between their two countries for centuries. India has also had some influence on some of the areas in and near China.

Human Environment Interaction

Dr. Hans Petermann says that Japan needs to go all solar and natural gas energy for now until a fusion energy reactors can be built which are very safe, reliable and there are no toxic wastes like the billions of tons of nuclear waste that are already being disposed of throughout the world. They are storing the nuclear waste at Yucca Flats Nevada U.S.A. With the Fusion Energy process that will exclude the toxins altogether.

The nuclear waste can be made inert by using brown's gas to neutralize the nuclear waste totally. Dr. Hans Petermann knew Dr. Yull Brown he was originally from Bulgaria.

China must now reverse their damages that they have caused into the earth's atmosphere. They can begin doing research to find out how best to do so but they must also drastically reduce and further limit their industrial and agricultural pollutants. If they want to continue to operate any of their industrial plants they must now convert to the steam engine to produce energy because this will not produce any toxins to the environment. They must now convert to the steam engine.

A highly nuclear radioactive fuel rod from nuclear reactors will remain radioactive for thousands of years if not millennia and must be stored in remote places where they will not contaminate water, air, or any other parts of the eco system's environment.

In all of man's genius inventions we still have not found out how to enjoy this life and be productive by being 100% renewable, recyclable, or reusable. And until life becomes uninhabitable on planet earth or mankind wises up to the fact that is the only way to survive on this planet is by not producing things that you cannot live with or get rid of for thousands of years.

The truth is... nuclear energy should have never been produced. Neither should plastic have ever been produced. But we did and now we need to fix it. Either find the antidote or stop producing it whatever the disease, or in this case toxin may be.

In the last 200 years population growth has increased by fourfold going from 1.5 billion to 6 billion in the 20th century alone. Now it is 7 billion since we are in the 21st century. Because of the mass population growth that translates into the greater environmental changes that are likely to occur.

 This is all the more reason we need new international limits on toxins and new international legislation on proper waste management, and new regulations on how things are to be disposed of and what can or cannot be disposed.

Who is responsible for chemical, biological or nuclear toxins being released in the environment wreaking havoc of Fukushima Nuclear waste pouring into the ocean, oil spills in the gulf, detergents used in the gulf to clean up the oil spills or the pesticides, hormones, and antibodies used in agriculture?   Where is the proper waste management?

Poor countries should not be allowed to sale landfills to other countries unless there are stipulations included that prohibit open and unsanitary garbage dumps.

We must drastically reduce the amount of waste that is being produced.

References:

http://upload.wikimedia.org/wikipedia/commons/a/ac/India_mineral_map.jpg

http://maps.unomaha.edu/Peterson/geog1000/MapLinks/Japan.htm

http://en.wikipedia.org/wiki/Pollution_in_China

http://beforeitsnews.com/war-and-conflict/2012/06/a-burmese-solution-to-beijings- south-china-sea-behavior-2279146.html

http://en.wikipedia.org/wiki/Natural_resources_of_India

http://www.eia.gov/countries/country-data.cfm?fips=ja

http://www.businessinsider.com/russia-china-pipeline-2014-5

Dr. Hans Petermann
760-327-4761
P.O. BOX 74
Palm Springs, CA. 92263

Climate Change & Human Environment

A highly nuclear radioactive fuel rod from nuclear reactors will remain radioactive for thousands of years if not millennia and must be stored in remote places where they will not contaminate water, air, or any other parts of the eco system's environment.

In all of man's genius inventions we still have not found out how to enjoy this life and be productive by being 100% renewable, recyclable, or reusable. And until life becomes uninhabitable on planet earth or mankind wises up to the fact that is the only way to survive on this planet is by not producing things that you cannot live with or get rid of for thousands of years then generation after generation will be stuck with their forefathers junk.

The truth is... nuclear energy should have never been produced. Neither should plastic have ever been produced. But we did now we need to fix it. Either find the antidote or stop producing it whatever the disease, or in this case toxin may be.
 #green #sustainable #ecofriendly

Wonder if that is why all the starfish are dying by the millions? http://www.dailymail.co.uk/news/article-2550621/MILLIONS-starfish-mysteriously-dying-North-Americas-west-coast.html

One way to get closer to being 100% renewable, recyclable, or reusable is the way that I do it: I've been doing this proficiently for many years now. The only thing that I dispose of that cannot be recycled are things like dirty Q-tips, napkins, paper towels, toilet paper, tea bags, or food particles. Everything else gets recycled, reused or renewed in one way or another. http://education.nationalgeographic.com/education/encyclopedia/great-pacific-garbage-patch/?ar_a=1

Mindful Waste

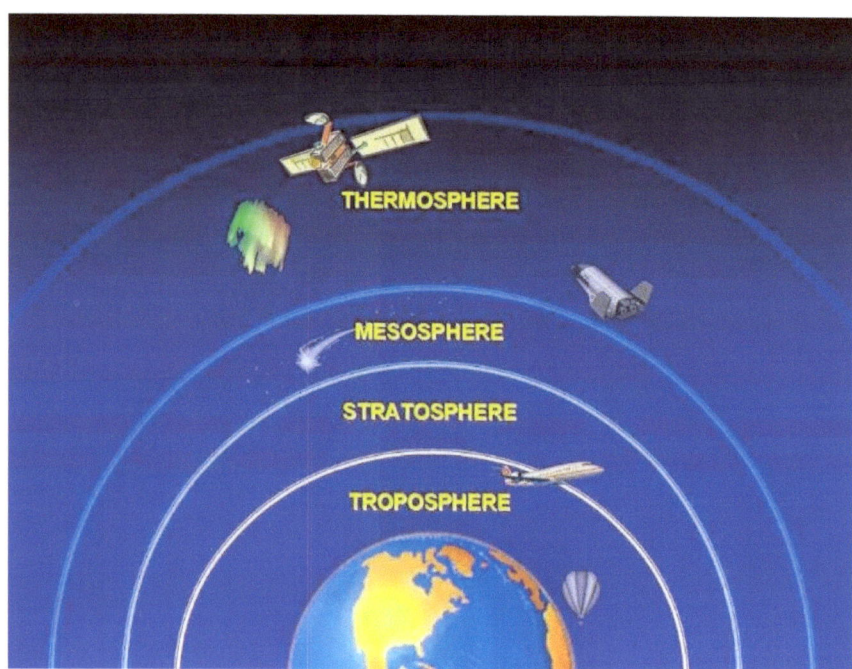

In the last 200 years population growth has increased by four times going from 1 and 1/2 billion to 6 billion in the 20th century alone. Now it is 7 billion since we are in the 21st century. Because of the mass population growth that translates into the greater environmental changes that are likely to occur.

 This is all the more reason we need new international limits on toxins and new international legislation on proper waste management, and new regulations on how things are to be disposed of and what can or cannot be disposed.

Poor countries should not be allowed to sale landfills to other countries unless there are stipulations included that prohibit open and unsanitary garbage dumps.
We must drastically reduce the amount of waste that is being produced.

Perhaps there could be another action similar to the Vienna Convention where the Montreal Protocol international agreement was signed in 1987 by 105 countries and the European Community which stopped the ozone layers fast depletion by aerosol sprays and refrigerants.

It is TIME for America and China to sign the Kyoto Agreement Protocol and strengthen the Copenhagen Accord Agreement

 http://en.wikipedia.org/wiki/Kyoto_Protocol

http://en.wikipedia.org/wiki/Copenhagen_Accord

http://globalriskinsights.com/

https://maplecroft.com/themes/gr/

http://www.weforum.org/issues/global-risks

http://www.un.org/geninfo/bp/enviro.html

http://www.unep.org/Documents.multilingual/Default.asp?DocumentID=55&ArticleID=274&l=en

http://www.thegef.org/gef/

 #green #sustainable #ecofriendly

Wonder why all the starfish are dying by the millions? They now say is is because of a virus. Could it be possible that the virus was initiated by all the pollution?

 http://www.dailymail.co.uk/news/article-2550621/MILLIONS-starfish-mysteriously-dying-North-Americas-west-coast.html

One way to get closer to being 100% renewable, recyclable, or reusable is the way that I do it: I've been doing this proficiently for many years now. The only thing that I dispose of that cannot be recycled are things like dirty Q-tips, napkins, paper towels, toilet paper, tea bags, or items that cannot be washed and have food particles on it.

My cans, jars and bottles get cycled through the dishwasher before I recycle them making it easier for the recycle process and that way I can store the recycling in my house without any odor. Everything else gets recycled, reused or renewed in one way or another. I use my tiny applesauce containers as mini ice trays.

One applesauce container is perfect for one glass of water. You only need that one ice cube. Other items that have lids to them are perfect to keep for food storage or even dried herbs or powdered herbs.
 http://education.nationalgeographic.com/education/encyclopedia/great-pacific-garbage-patch/?ar_a=1

Geographical Agriculture Diffusion

I am a vegetarian more than 75% of the time with the exception of Passover, Thanksgiving, Christmas and a few blue moons a year when I take out fast food so I would say that most of the products that I consume have been effected by the geographical agriculture theme of movement.

My favorite food is the avocado which has its agriculture hearth in the East and highlands of Mexico. I also love the potato and recently the potato was discovered to provide a lot of antioxidants that are beneficial in fighting carcinogenic like the fertilizers and pesticides called "Roundup" produced by a company mentioned in the book named Monsanto.

On that note I will share a bit of home economics with you; when you buy any fruits, vegetables and even beans or lentils it is important that you wash the food well with salt and water.

It is strange how some related the tubular potato to a disease and others thought that tomatoes were poisonous before one brave soul ventured off into the edible fruit and not a vegetable.

It is the only one from its nightshade family that is not poisonous. Avocado's and tomatoes are very easy to grow right here in California where I live. Avocados also grow very easily in Florida but the taste is distinctly different and I really don't care for the Florida avocado at all.

Tomatoes can even grow from an upside down planter where the dirt is on top and the tomato plant comes out of the bottom of the planter and grows upward producing first little yellow fragile flowers with a wonderful aroma of fresh tomatoes.

The bible actually speaks of rams that come from Bashan in Deuteronomy 32:15 "Butter of the herd, and milk of the flock, with the fat of lambs, (I recently enjoyed the delicious Passover Roasted Shank as I do each year) rams from Bashan, and goats, with the choicest grains of wheat, and of the blood of the grape thou drankest wine" It also mentions eating honey and oil from the crag.

I am thankful for the tea that was brought over from East India during the Boston Tea Party when American's dressed as Indians were outraged because of the British "Tea Act" May 10, 1773. I drink tea every day. I love black tea, green tea, rooibos tea, and chai. I also drink herbal teas such as Senna, ginger, licorice and I know many of these herbs are not native to the American soil.

I am thankful for having such a great variety that the colonizers first embarked on creating a path for us to have access for other cultural fruits, vegetables, roots, teas, and meats.

5 Main Themes Of San Diego Metropolitan Geography

San Diego Metropolitan Reflections Essay

Author Kimmy Nelson

Spring 2014 Geog 200 D02

The Five Main Themes of geography of San Diego and her suburban city of La Mesa

1.   Location –Latitude and Longitude

2.   Place –What is it like there

3.   Movement –People, Ideas, Goods moving from one place to another

4.   Region—A Group Of Places that have any human or physical characteristics in common

5. Human Environmental Interaction—Humans Adapt To Environment or Effect The Environment

  Five Themes Of Geography For San Diego and Her Suburban City of La Mesa

Location

San Diego Metropolitan Area

The port of San Diego, CA. is home to our navy is Latitude, 32°44'8" North and Longitude, 117°10'36" West. The Chargers play at Qualcomm Stadium which has it's own Trolley exit called "Qualcomm Stadium" headquartered in Chargers Park. San Diego, CA. is in the South--Western Hemisphere of The United States of America. San Diego is a border city as it is on the Northern border of Mexico on the West Coast in America. La Mesa, CA. is only a ten miles North East of San Diego, CA.

Place

Southern California

San Diego and her suburb city of La Mesa, CA. are some of the finest areas that Southern California has to offer. San Diego is the home of the National Football Team the San Diego Chargers. San Diego is also home to the United States Navy since 1918 with 54 ships and 13 piers. The Chargers moved to San Diego in 1961 and in 1970 they had the AFL-NFL merger after winning the AFC four times.

Movement

Distribution and Mobility

We have the best public transportation system that anyone could ever hope for with the Metropolitan Transit System of buses, trains and trolleys that are all connected at many different locations and times throughout the regions of San Diego and her suburban areas. There are also boats and shipping vessels all along the bay and port areas along the coastal shores and waterways. There is also a ferry that will carry your vehicle across the water. San Diego has a huge airport where many people fly to as it is the main airport South of Los Angeles, CA. Pedestrians and bikers travel along the sidewalks and roads throughout San Diego and La Mesa too.

Culture & Surroundings

In 2012 the statistics from the San Diego County Census Bureau reported that the White population to be 76.6% and that the black or African American population to be 5.6% while the Native American Indian were only 1.3% in population. The Asian population was 11.6% of the population and Hawaiian and other Pacific Islanders were only .06% of the population.

Two or more races present in the households were 4.2%. Hispanic was 32.7% in population and the White alone not Hispanic or Latino were 47.6% in population. While 49.7% are female in gender, less than 6.7% are children under five years old and less than 23% are teenagers under eighteen years of age.
And 12% are 65 years of age or older male or females living in San Diego County. 83% have lived in the same house for over one year 2008-2012. 23.2% are foreign born persons 2008-2012 and 37.1% use another language where they reside other than English 2008-2012.

85.4% are High School Graduates 2008-2012, 34% have a Bachelor's Degree between 2008-2012 and over 230, 000 Veterans between 2008 and 2012. 54.5% home ownership 2008-2012 and approximately $30, 683.00 per capita in the past twelve months 2008-2012.

As you can see we are a very diverse culture with a lot to offer. And as one of the world's top twelve highest earning agriculture environments is all the more reason why it is a very important global region.

And even with the statistics previously mentioned there are still 13.9% of our population that are listed as below poverty income between 2008 and 2012. In 2008 the city of San Diego was reported to be one of the top ten safest cities with populations over 100,000 persons. In 2010 the city of San Diego was listed as one of the top ten highest crime and unsafe cities with populations over 100,000 persons.

This could be attributed to the drug war crossing over into America from Mexico. I believe that our local government is as much responsible for our border security as the Federal government because no one cares about their own neighborhood as much as the person who lives there.

The Federal government in large does not have to deal with having their purse stole, their identity stole or a violent gang member who is lawless. Nor do they have to worry about the gang member who watches to see when you leave your home so that they can illegally enter at their own liberty.

We have a rich military history here in San Diego with the navy using our ports as home base. And the military have a wonderful community nearby the ports where they have their own little close knit communities of mothers and children and wives or spouses of our United States Military.

Region

Climate

The climate here is somewhat tropical throughout Southern California so it is lush with green shrubs, ivy, and beautiful flowers scattered throughout like a tapestry landscape in between the buildings and the highways. There are also lots of avocado farms, orange groves, almond trees, and grape vines where large quantities of fruits and vegetables are grown and harvested annually as San Diego is home to the twelfth largest crop producing area in our state. The entire Region South of Los Angeles share the same climate and temperature on a daily basis. There are occasional winds and sometimes there are droughts. We have occasional earthquakes throughout the entire region of California but it is our climate that separates us from the rest of the state. As San Diego has perfect temperatures all year round that is suitable for human life and sustainability.

Human Environmental Interactions

Transportation and Architecture

Fishing boats, fisheries and lots of seafood restaurants that are connected to the seafood industry have had quite an impact on the sea life environment. The freeways, interstates, railroad tracks and buildings in mass numbers in this dense population have also had a great effect on the environment making everything much more accessible.

Earth's Dynamics

The earthquake prone tectonic plates, the fire prone mountains and forests along with the mudslide prone hills in the San Diego area have also had an effect on the way that people build businesses and homes and even the way that insurance is sold or distributed because they must take in considerations those likely scenarios before they can build or issue an insurance policy.

Green House Gas Emissions

The greenhouse gases and ocean pollution have now caught the attention of the world as to how vitally important the coral reefs are to human survival so that there are now some efforts to clean up the mess that we've made. Just off the coast of San Diego there is a Plastic Vortex floating that is the size of two states of Texas where plastic hovers above the ocean's surface on the waves and even beneath the surface a few feet deep. It is disposed garbage that somehow found its way to the ocean and has polluted and killed much of the ocean life. Some are working on solutions how to clean it up and prevent it from happening again.

References

1. http://quickfacts.census.gov/qfd/states/06/06073.html

2. http://geography.about.com/od/teachgeography/a/5themes.htm

3. http://en.wikipedia.org/wiki/Plate_tectonics

4. http://en.wikipedia.org/wiki/Great_Pacific_garbage_patch

Naming Only A Fraction Of The Implications On Earth From Extracting Energy Resources

Now that Putin and China have a pipeline deal that will transport energy from Russia to China Putin can take advantage of this to leverage power in the world. Wars have been fought throughout time over resources. Nations have been plumaged and ravished over energy.

Independence from other nations resources would be idea but if that is not possible than this sort of leverage gets asserted. But not without global risks of pollution or other consequences from tampering with the natural structure of the earth's surface and resources that are deep beneath.

In May, 2014 there was another oil spill but this time it was only 50,000 gallons and they all landed on the streets of Los Angeles. This time it wasn't because of an offshore accident or a train wreck, or even a diesel spill. The oil pipes beneath earth's surface burst causing oil to spew into the atmosphere above the city of Los Angeles then fall back to the ground and run like a river in the streets below.

It was also in May 2014 that the Scientists released documentation linking the groundwater pumping to the increased earth quake activity near the San Andreas Fault line.

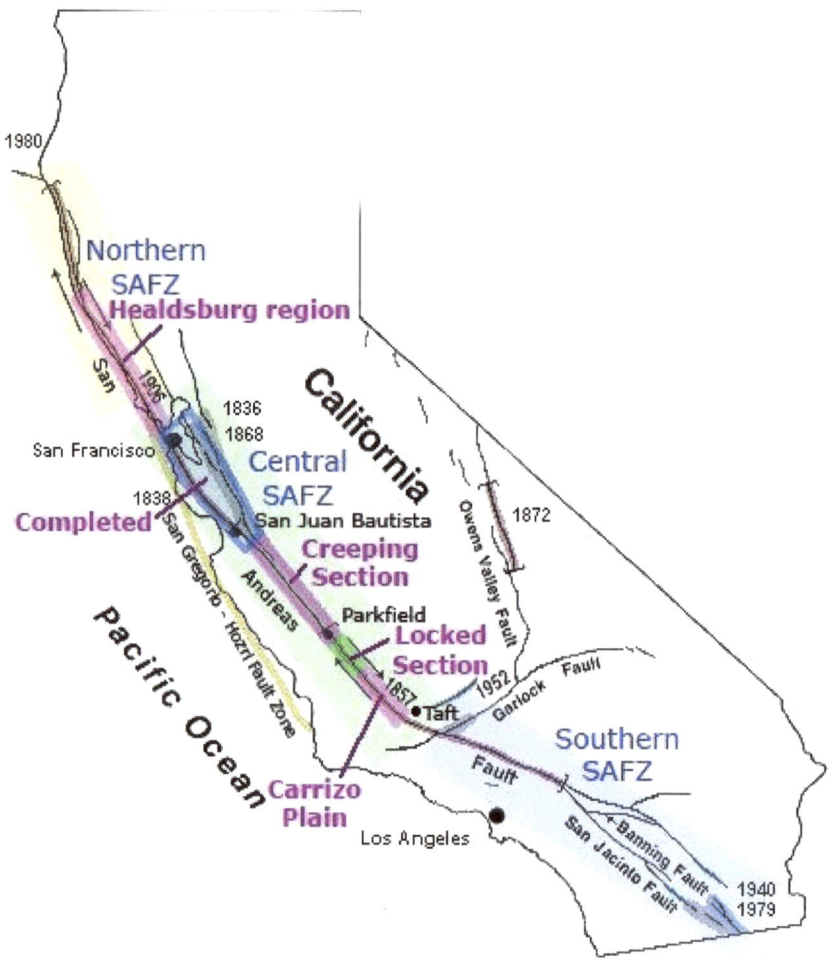

Study reports say "These results suggest that human activity may give rise to a gradual increase in the rate of earthquake occurrence," It was published in the Journal Nature May 2014 written by scientists from Western Washington University, University of Ottawa, University of Nevada, Reno and UC Berkeley.

There needs to be a global monitoring system that polices the pollutants and dangers put forth by the chemicals of any sort and the implications that they have on the earth. There also needs to be global taxing or tariffs on companies and countries who cause damage to earth's surface or below her ocean's floor surface because the damages are virtually irreparable and will cost us all when there is no more oxygen, food or clean water.

If I (a Native American Indian) were to illegally cross over into Canada I would hope that they would arrest me... Unless of course they don't care! How do people all over this have the guts to illegally enter other lands and countries without the proper legal documentation...? It is simply wrong to break the law no matter whose law it is! It is too dangerous, there are too many diseases and too many terrorists to allow that to go on in Democracies or freedom loving countries anywhere.

http://www.judicialwatch.org/blog/2014/07/illegal-alien-minors-spreading-tb-ebola-dengue-swine-flu/

http://www.foxnews.com/us/2011/03/22/report-13-illegal-immigrants-apprehended-marine-uniforms/

If the Hispanics, Haitians, Filipinos or any other people want to come to America to work or go to school that is another world story. Let them live here among us on a temporary visa until they can get the permanent visa. But don't illegally enter our country. I don't think it is good that they should be allowed to illegally enter other people's countries in the UK either. I think both countries should be held accountable for its citizens that decide to break the law. There should be repercussions on both sides of the border.

Reference

http://www.businessinsider.com/oil-pipe-bursts-in-atwater-village-california-2014-5

http://www.latimes.com/local/lanow/la-me-ln-groundwater-more-earthquakes-20140514-story.html

Putin's Pipeline Deal With China

Putin wants to become the world's energy king but the current sanctions that Europe has on Russia until they respect the Ukraine's independence will continue to cause the roubel to lose value. (Some links made visible for those who are reading the not digital version.)
http://www.theguardian.com/world/2014/nov/14/putin-russia-oil-price-collapse-sanctions-g20

Putin has signed the Minsk agreement that calls for a ceasefire in the Ukraine. However David Cameron said that the current sanctions will still stand.
http://www.theguardian.com/world/2014/sep/05/ukraine-ceasefire-east-minsk-peace-talks

With the increased flow of oil to China for more crude oil Russia is still under contract agreement to honor PKN Orlen, Rosenft that they will supply as much as 8.28

million tons of crude to Unipetrol RPA under a three year contract until June 2016 valued at 6.1 billion dollars. http://www.bloomberg.com/news/2013-06-20/rosneft-plans-60-billion-oil-supply-deal-with-china-putin-says.html

Chinese delegates Deputy Prime Minister Zhang Gaoli signed an agreement in April of 2014 with Rosneft to deliver thirty seven million metric tons of oil annually measuring up to 743,000 barrels a day to China National Petroleum Company beginning in 2010.

Rosneft is going to supply some crude oil through the East Siberian Pacific Ocean and it will be an increase of only 800,000 tons added to the 15 million. http://rt.com/business/184176-russia-china-gas-siberian-power/

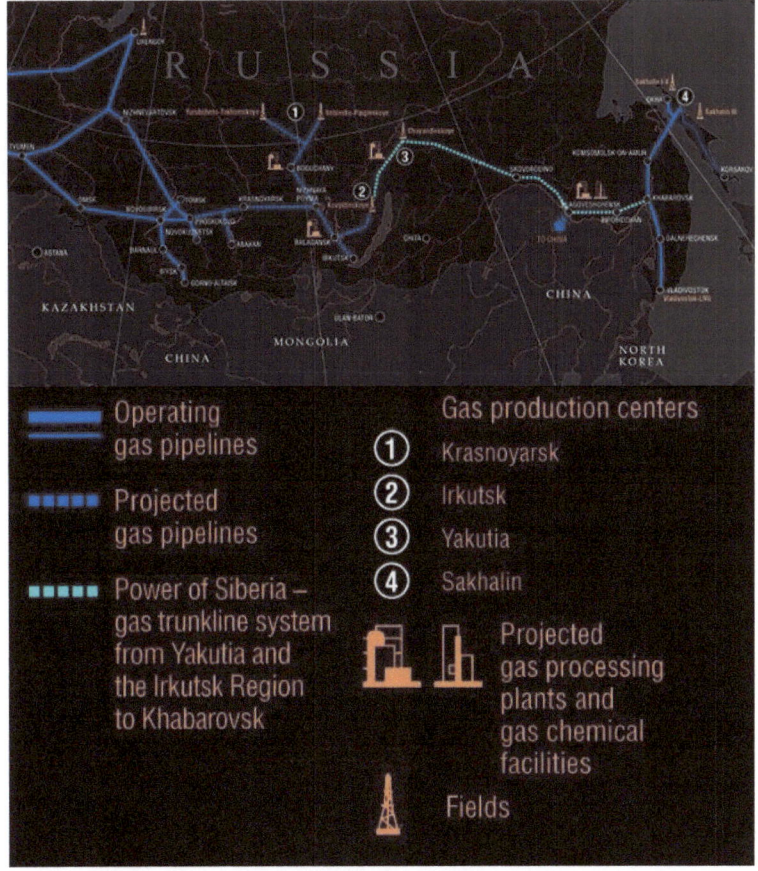

China's imports of 50 million tons per year "isn't attainable" said Chief Executive Officer Igor Sechin.

China has big plans for that oil as they are hitting Brazil up for $3.2 billion to purchase Jets, energy, and cars. China also pledged up to 8 billion for other expenditures such as securing loans for Brazil. http://www.bloomberg.com/news/2014-07-17/xi-visit-brings-brazil-chinese-loans-and-jet-aircraft-purchases.html

CHINA'S NUCLEAR POWER

China also have 50 to 75 "nuclear capable intercontinental ballistic missiles (ICBMs) that could reach the US. Within the next 15 years, China will likely have an arsenal of over 100 ICBMs." Jeremy Bender

Read more: http://www.businessinsider.com/chinas-nuclear-capabilities-increasing-2014-11#ixzz3JoMs2lfc

So it doesn't appear that China is at all interested in creating a healthy atmosphere with less emissions.

KEYSTONE

Keystone failed to pass yet again after the General Elections of November 2014 but only by a one vote deficit. However, with the newly attained Republican seats to the Senate they are sure to pass it at the beginning of the New Year in 2015.

This will reduce gas prices even further and open up much needed jobs for unemployed Americans but only at the expense of the global environment and those whose lands and lives will be effected.

Only the environmentalists seem to be the ones that oppose this project. That is likely because of the unemployment rates high since 2008 causing a terrible effects to the housing and auto industry.

The American infrastructure is a much more needed project as water mains have been breaking all over this country wreaking havoc on cars, homes and businesses from North East part of the country to Kansas City to Texas, from Texas to California and as was reported in the Oil pipes bursting in Los Angeles in May of 2014, the water pipes bursting all over Texas due to the drought in 2011

http://www.examiner.com/article/so-many-massive-water-main-breaks-jul-1-aug-12-more-new-normal-you-bet

http://stateimpact.npr.org/texas/tag/drought/

But many are more interested in building this pipeline to run oil than they are to build infrastructure that will run much needed life sustaining water to the lives, homes and businesses all across America but that does not seem to draw as much attention to Congress or to the American people as the money making Keystone pipeline.

Yet, each Spring many countries flood due to snow and ice melting and subterranean drainage but few areas have learned to channel that water to a storage reservoir basins for usage.

http://www.blm.gov/ca/st/en/fo/palmsprings/wilderness/big _maria_mountains.html

In some areas it is so bad every year that in 2011 the army Corps of engineers were forced to blow up levees that flooded nearby corn fields in order to save nearby cities.

http://thinkprogress.org/climate/2011/05/03/208016/floods-army-corps-levee/ Army Corps Blow Levee

http://en.wikipedia.org/wiki/Mississippi_River Mississippi River

Yet that same year only two months later a terrible drought was happening. But everyone is so interested in piping oil they have not even considered piping the subterranean drainage from Red River or Mississippi River or Washington State flooding or Nashville flooding and piping it to the drought prone areas of Texas and California.

http://www.ndsu.nodak.edu/fargoflood/ Red River Floods

http://www.npr.org/blogs/thesalt/2014/11/14/360126699/str ategies-help-calif-ranchers-farmers-weather-drought California drought

http://en.wikipedia.org/wiki/2010_Tennessee_floods
Nashville Flood too

http://www.ecy.wa.gov/programs/sea/floods/flooding_wa_s
tate.html Washington State Flooding

https://www.tceq.texas.gov/response/drought Texas
drought

Maybe one day food and water will be as valuable as oil
and they will figure out how o route the mountain drainage,
the snow and ice melting waters and the subterranean
drainage to drought stricken farm lands.

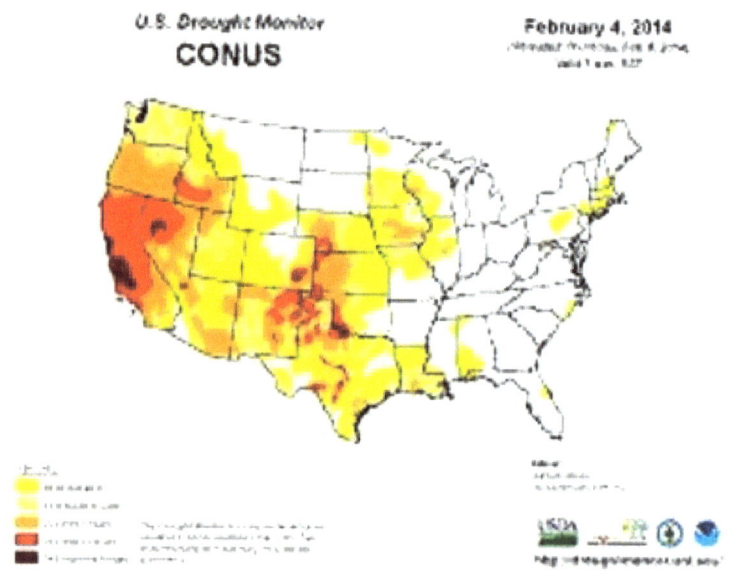

Small produce and small crops are only part of the result from the drought stricken farm lands in California and all over the world.

Livestock and perished too and I personally find this to be not only the farmers fault but the states fault for not helping the farmers to save their livestock.

www.ingramcontent.com/pod-product-compliance
Lightning Source LLC
Chambersburg PA
CBHW050835290526
45792CB00001B/403